My Favourite STORIES of Values

DS PUBLISHERS (INDIA)

Tel : +91 (11) 6525 3158, 4156 3757
E-mail : ds_bookmaster@yahoo.co.in

the Bookmaster
CLASSIC SERIES

My Favourite
STORIES OF VALUES

Compiled by
Vimla Kaul

Illustrated by
Kiran Art Studio

ISBN 978 81 87131 81 6

Cover designed by
Lovika Arts

Processed at
Lipee Scan Pvt. Ltd.

Printed at
Haploos Printing House

PREFACE

In these days of loss of values of life and living, it was considered a matter of concern that, we must make an attempt to imbibe these values at the budding stage of the children. With this concern in view, short, interesting and simple stories have been collected in this book for children to enjoy, understand and assimilate.

Stories are the most interesting medium through which children understand depths of truth and also take the truths in, to the depths of their heads and hearts. Once they get this medium of instruction, they get so encrossed in it wholeheartedly that they are able to sip the nectar there of.

The author believes that, values imbibed at this budding stage of life get seeped into the depths of the being. No matter what happens to the adult in later life he/she will never be able to shake of these values from his/her system. The values are so deeply embedded in his being that they become a part of his physical and mental existence.

Thus it is felt that, this is the right time of the world's needs and the opportune moment of the child's life that, these little stories should be taken help of. If we start from this early stage of life, at least, the next generation we produce may be of values befitting good human beings. With this objective in view the author has got together this little ensemble of short stories for little children. It is hoped that, the children will enjoy and cherish these stories and, parents and teachers are able to give a new direction to values in the children. At this point, a suggestion will be given to all elders concerned, i.e. we have to give good example to children if at all we expect the desired results.

Wishing you all a happy reading and an enjoyable time with this new book.

V. Kaul

CONTENTS

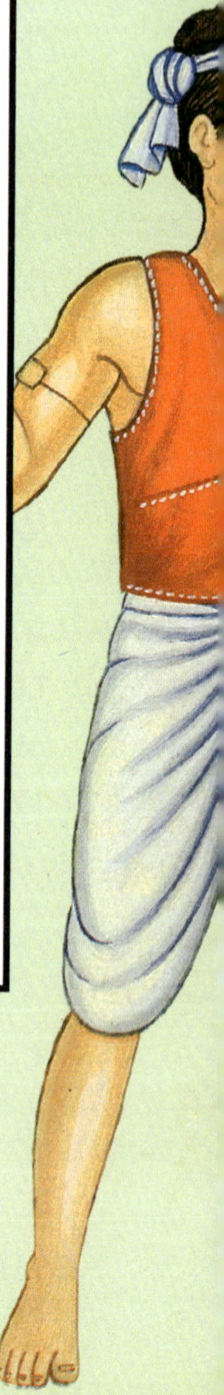

CONTENTS

Adam and Eve

God was very happy after HE had made the Universe.

God made the Universe

God made Adam

After making the Universe, God wanted to make it full of life. So, HE made the first man whose name was Adam. This man, Adam, was as good as God himself.

Now after making man, God, kind as He is, made a nice home for this Man. This was a beautiful garden called the Eden Garden.

Now Adam had a beautiful home to live in, but he was alone. This was felt by God also, and, kind as God is, He gave man a friend. Now God made the first woman, whom He called Eve.

Man's home was now ready in its full splendour, with a man, a woman, and a beautiful home to live in.

God made Eve

When God gave the home of Eden Garden to Adam and Eve, he told them to eat any fruit they wanted to. But, God showed them one tree and said to them, "Do not eat the fruit of that tree".

The forbidden fruit

For a long time, both Adam and Eve obeyed God, and did not eat the fruit God had told them not to, and they lived very happily together in their home, the Eden Garden.

One day, it so happened, that, Eve was walking in the garden, and a serpent came and stood near her.

The serpent tempts

This serpent spoke to Eve, and told her to eat the fruit that God had told her not to. Eve thought for a moment and then got tempted and plucked the forbidden fruit.

Eve plucked one and started eating it and Oh! She liked it, as, it was very sweet.

Soon God came to know that, Eve had eaten the forbidden fruit, and disobeyed Him. She had taken it herself and also gave it to Adam. With this, God was very angry, and he punished them.

Eve disobeys

The punishment God gave to Adam and Eve was that, they both had to leave their beautiful home, the Eden Garden, and come down to Earth. From then on, this Earth became man's home instead of EDEN GARDEN. God punished man for not obeying.

THE FIRST THING FOR US TO LEARN IS-TO OBEY.

The Great Prince Rama

God wants us all to obey our parents and all elders. He gave us an example of obedience, when he came to earth like us. There was once a prince by the name of Rama. Rama was the son of a king whose name was Dashratha. Rama lived in a palace with his parents and three other brothers.

Rama living happily in the palace

Rama gets married

When Rama grew up to be a young man, he got married to a princess whose name was Sita.

After their marriage, Rama and Sita lived very happily with the other members of the family. However, after a few happy days together in the palace, one day, came a test for the young boy Rama. Rama's father called the son, and ordered Rama to go out from his home palace, and spend fourteen years in the forest. Rama was ordered to go and live in the forest for fourteen years.

Rama taking orders

Rama obeys

The young prince Rama who had always lived in the palace, did not once ask his father why he was ordered to do so, but obeyed at once.

Rama goes to the forest

See, how readily Rama obeyed his father. He never asked any question and just went only because his father wanted him to do so.

OBEDIENCE IS A GREAT VIRTUE.

The Greedy Lion

One day, in the jungle, a lion saw a beautiful little lamb, and he wanted to eat it. Just as he was thinking of the plan to eat the lamb saying to himself, "That lamb will make a good dinner", he saw a deer pass by from just there.

Lion looking at his food

The lion trying for a better dinner

Seeing the deer who was at some distance, the lion said to himself, “This will be a better dinner”. Saying so, the lion left the lamb and ran after the deer. However the deer who runs very fast, was soon out of the sight of the lion.

Soon the lion saw that, he would not be able to chase and catch the fast deer, and so decided to return to where the lamb was.

The lion returns

I wanted too much so I have nothing

When the lion came back, the lamb had gone away to safety, and so, the lion was left hungry. He tried for more and better so, he lost the little he had.

IT IS NOT GOOD TO BE GREEDY, BECAUSE IT MAKES US LOSE WHAT WE HAVE.

THE PROUD PEACOCK

Once upon a time, there was a peacock who had a good friend, a crane. They were both very happy with each other, and life was moving very smoothly and merrily.

Now it used to happen very often that, the peacock heard several people praising it for its unusual beauty. When he heard it very often, he started feeling the pride for his beauty. One day, this pride got into the peacock's head, and he told his friend the crane, "Friend, I am robed like a king, in gold and purple, while you, you have no colour on your wings".

Aha - see how beautiful I really am

The crane flying off to the heavens

Hearing this, the crane felt very hurt but, he replied very wisely to the peacock. The crane said, "Yes dear friend, you are very beautiful but, God's gift to me is no less. I fly to the heights of Heaven and sing to the Heavens above, while, you walk on earth like a cock or like any other bird".

From that day the friendship of the peacock and the crane was broken. Never be proud for if, you are so proud you will lose good friends. When you have something good be happy for it but, do not be proud of it.

WE BECOME PROUD WHEN WE HEAR TOO MUCH OF PRAISE. IT IS NOT GOOD TO BE PROUD.

THE BOYS AND THE FROG

One day, some boys were playing near a pond. Inside the water of the pond, they saw a lot of frogs.

Seeing the frogs in the water, the children left their play. They started picking some stones, and aiming and hitting the frogs. This became their game.

The sport of the boys

A lesson from a frog

In this game, the boys went on hurting many frogs, while some were hurt very badly. Seeing this sport for a long time, and watching so many frogs being hurt, at last, one big frog got out of the pond. He said, “Friends, what is game for you, is misery for us. Please try to find some other game to play in which you do not hurt others”.

Hearing this, the boys felt very sad, and they said, “Sorry friends, we did not understand that our game was trouble for you all, we will not do this again”.

EVEN A LESSER BEING CAN TEACH.

NEVER TELL A LIE

Once upon a time, there was a man whose name was Peter. He went to a far off place in search of work, to earn a livelihood.

Peter out to look for work

He reached a far off town, and got some work there. In this town, he stayed for one year. As he had earned enough now, he wanted to go back home. He came back to his town. Here, he started talking a lot about the town where he had worked for one year. Soon enough, people got tired of hearing his talks of work and all that he had learnt.

Peter talking about his visit

One day, Peter told his friends, that, in the new town he had been he could jump very well-and one day he said, "I showed them all that, I jump better than all of them".

He continued, "I jumped highest of them all". Hearing this, one man from the crowd shouted aloud, "Peter, show us how well and high you jump". Hearing this, Peter ran away from the crowd, and never again did he boast of what all he did in the new town. He knew that, he was telling a

People who boast are found out

lie, and that, if people came to know about his lies, they would never again believe what ever he said.

WE SHOULD NEVER TELL LIES-IT HARMS US BY GETTING INSULTS FROM ALL.

SERVICE IS LOVE

When we have love for someone, we must be able to show it to him/her. Now, the question that arises is that, how to show this love. The best and most honest way of showing love, is by serving the one you love - for, service is love.

Once upon a time there was a young boy whose name was Bhai Laiha, and he was very fond of serving his master. One day it so happened that, the master cut three bundles of grass, and asked his sons to carry them home.

Sons of the master being asked to carry grass

The angry father

The master asked his sons to take the bundles to their home but, the children refused to take them as,they thought this was a low task for the sons of the master to perform. While these people were still talking about the task, Bhai Laiha happened to come there.

Bhai Laiha asked the master, “What is the matter Sir”? To this, the master replied in disgust, “Bhai Laiha, see these sons of mine are not willing to carry these bundles of grass. They say that, they are the sons of the master, and so, how can they do such lowly work? I am too old to carry this load so, I do not know what I should do with this grass”.

I am always ready to serve

Hearing this, Bhai Laiha at once picked up all the three bundles of grass, and walked off to the master's home.

With this action of Bhai Laiha, the master was very happy, and was also very proud of him.

Bhai Laiha used to do such work for all the people of his village. This is why, he was very popular and loved in the village. He was loved because he served all, and showed his love for all men.

SERVICE TO MAN IS LOVE OF MAN

THE HARE AND THE TORTOISE

Once upon a time there were two friends, a tortoise and a hare. Thcy were happy with each other, liked each other, and played with each other. The hare is a fast moving creature and the tortoise, the opposite, very slow.

One day it so happened that, another hare came that way. He asked his like, the other hare, “Hello friend, how do you remain friends with this tortoise. He is so slow, don’t you get irritated with his slow movements”? The Hare started really wondering why he was a friend to such a slow mover.

After some thought the hare, the tortoise’s friend got

The two friends

an idea. He told the tortoise, "To-day, let us have a race. The one who wins the race will always be the senior friend between the two of us." The tortoise agreed to the plan. They fixed a certain point of victory. They both planned out the detail and started off at once.

The race was between two unequals, and the hare was sure that he would be the winner. Being sure of his victory against the slow tortoise, the hare moved with great confidence. After the hare had moved for sometime, he thought, "the tortoise must be far behind from me, come on, let me have a nap for sometime". Saying this to himself, the hare slept under the shade of a tree. After sometime, the slow but steady tortoise reached this place, and saw the hare resting. He felt that he, being much slower could not afford to take any rest. The tortoise thus continued on his way, without giving a moment's break.

The tortoise continued to move ahead. On the other hand, the hare slept for some more time. When the hare got up from sleep, he realised that, he had slept for a long time, and wondered where the tortoise would be. Now the

The tortoise moves ahead

The winner - the tortoise

hare ran as fast as he could. After a long run, the hare at last reached the fixed place - and what did he see. Ah! The slow but steady tortoise had already reached the place. The slow tortoise had won the race. Now onwards, the tortoise would be the senior partner in their friendship.

WE MUST BE STEADY IN WORK- BECAUSE A STEADY WORKER WINS.

GOD WILL PUNISH THE EVIL

Once upon a time there was a farmer. He sowed good seeds in his field and expected a good harvest of wheat in his field.

This good farmer had some enemies, who wanted to make the farmer unhappy and lose money on his harvest. At night time, once, these enemies thought of a plan. When the farmer was asleep at night, they came to the good

The farmer sowing seeds

Tares being sown

farmer's field and sowed tares among the wheat and went away.

After sometime when the wheat was ripened, there rose also the tares in the midst of the wheat.

This became a serious cause of worry to the farmer. If the rye grew with the wheat and was also cut and mixed with it, there may be a lot of sickness and even death may result.

Tares in the midst of wheat

God will punish the evil

The farmer to whom this field belonged was very worried so, he went to his master. The master told him that, this must be the work of some enemy. They all understood that, this was a very wicked thing being done by some bad person who was an enemy of the farmer. He said to the farmer, "You let the field come to full bloom then, the reaper of tares will gather the tares and they will be burnt. The wheat will be tied separately in bundles and stored in the barn.

Do you know what Jesus meant by this? He meant that, bad men and good men will grow together in this world. On the final day, the bad ones will be burnt and the good ones taken to God's home in Heaven.

The tares according to Jesus must be allowed to grow to their full size so that, the difference of evil and good becomes visible even to us people.

GOD WILL PUNISH THE EVIL BECAUSE HE WANTS ONLY GOOD TO EXIST IN THE WORLD.

I MUST BE HONEST

Once upon a time there was a village. The name of the village was Thampu. Near this village there was also a dense forest. In this village there lived one woodcutter, whose name was Satya.

Everyday, Satya who was a woodcutter used to go to the forest to cut wood. This wood he would bring to the village and sell it, to earn a living for his family.

The village of Thampu, and Satya in it

This woodcutter was in a funny habit. He used to go to the forest, and, after cutting some wood, he would start shouting aloud, for fun. In his loud shouts he used to say, “Save me friends, save me friends, a lion is here”.

Hearing this shout, all the people of the village would come to the forest to save him, but, what would they find- Satya just laughing and saying, Aha! I was only joking.

Seeing Satya safe and sound, the villagers would go back to the village. However, this became a habit for Satya, and he did this act of shouting for help, everyday. The villagers also came to help him every day. When after some time, one day when Satya was cutting wood in the forest, you know what happened?

The villagers come to help

The lion has come at last

That day, while Satya was busy cutting wood, the lion really did come.

Seeing the lion coming towards him, Satya climbed a tree, and started shouting for help as always before. The villagers all heard Satya shouting for help, but no one came that day. They said, "Oh he always shouts just for fun, to-day we will not go".

So, that day it was decided by all that no one will go to help, as, Satya just shouts for fun, and never is really in trouble. Now, Satya continued to sit on the top of the tree, and the lion waiting just under that tree, for its food-Satya.

After shouting for a long time, when no help came, Satya fell asleep on the branch of the tree.

The tired Satya asleep

Later on, in the night when Satya was fast asleep, he fell down from the tree, and got badly hurt. It was just luck that, by that time, the lion had left the spot.

Can you tell why no one came to help Satya the last time? This is because, they knew that he always tells lies. By telling lies all the time and never being honest, Satya had lost the trust of his friends in the village.

WE SHOULD NEVER TELL LIES EVEN IN A JOKE AS, BY THIS WE LOSE THE TRUST OF OUR OWN PEOPLE.

KRISHNA AND SUDAMA

Krishna had a very dear friend whose name was Sudama. When they were both children, they studied at the feet of the same Guru, at the Gurukul. Children, do you know what was the Gurukul? In the ancient times, in India, children did not go to schools for studies, like you all. The children used to go to the house of their Guru which was called the Gurukul. There, at the house of the Guru, they completed their studies.

Krishna and Sudama at the Gurukul

Krishna and Sudama studied at the feet of the same Guru, and, after completion of their studies, they both went to their homes.

Two friends in opposite states of life

As they both came to their houses, they got settled in their own different lives. Krishna became King of the country called Dwarka. On the other hand, Sudama got settled in the midst of abject poverty. It seemed that, the Goddess of poverty had taken a permanent abode in the house of Sudama. Sudama and his family, his wife and children did not even get enough to eat daily, and they wore torn clothes. Inspite of all this misery, Sudama never lost any opportunity of praising his old time friend Krishna.

After a long time in this misery, the wife of Sudama could not bear to see the sufferings of the little children, who were almost dying of hunger. One day she took the opportunity, and spoke to Sudama. She told him that, he was all the time in all praise of his friend Krishna. She said that she wondered how a friend of a king could be in such misery. She told Sudama, "I know dcar that you do not care for money but, for living we all need some money. Since you talk so much of your friend Krishna, and he happens to be a king also, I suggest that you go to him and ask him for any help that he can give".

This suggestion was, at first not liked by Sudama. He felt rather ashamed of going to seek for help from such a big man, and that also, for such a petty thing. However, his wife insisted that, Sudama should go in this condition to his friend and see how much help he can get. After long hours of persuasion, Sudama agreed to go and was glad that if nothing else was achieved, at least he would meet

Sudama's wife suggests help from Krishna

his dear friend. The next question that arose was, how could Sudama go to his friend's house without a gift. There was absolutely nothing in the poverty stricken house, to give as a gift to a king. However, his wife went to their neighbour's house and brought some rice, to be give to Krishna as a gift from Sudama. This rice was tied in a neat bundle, and at last, Sudama left for Dwarka.

Sudama set for Dwarka

When Sudama reached Dwarka, he was dazed to see the show of Dwarka. He asked for the king's palace, and went ahead. On reaching the palace, the gateman asked Sudama whom he wanted to meet in the palace. Sudama told the gateman that, he wanted to meet his very dear friend, the King himself - Shri Krishna. The gateman thought that this man was surely mad. How can a man wearing such torn clothes ever be a friend of our King. However as per the rules of the palace, the gateman made Sudama sit there, and he went inside the palace.

Dear friends meet after long

The moment Krishna heard the name of Sudama, his loved friend, he ran out towards the palace gate, and there he embraced Sudama, and tears of joy came trickling from the eyes of both the friends. The palace was as if thrown in a storm, and people thronged from everywhere to see these loving friends in a loving embrace. Sudama was taken inside the palace and entertained like a royal guest.

There was such a surprise in the minds of all, and they wondered how, a king could be such a dear friend of a beggar. They were all also surprised to see that, even after such a long time they had not forgotten each other, specially Krishna, who was a king.

Now do you understand who is a friend? You should call that person your friend who always loves you, no matter what happens.

A FRIEND IS A VERY BEAUTIFUL GIFT TO KEEP AND TREASURE.

THE VICTORIOUS BIRD GAURI

Once upon a time there was a girl whose name was Mary. Mary lived in a big house with her parents and brother and sisters. Since she was a big girl studying in senior school, she had a separate room for herself.

One day when Mary came back from her school, she found a little bird bringing straws in her room, to build a nest for herself. This, Mary did not like, as it made her room very dirty. Mary was very angry with the little bird, and the battle had started. Every day, the bird would bring straw to build the nest, and everyday, the girl would force it to get out of the room.

The battle is on

This war of nerves became a routine for Mary and the bird. The whole household came to know about it. However, it was so surprising to see that, inspite of so much opposition the bird continued her home-making project in Mary's room. This continued for quite a long time, with no sign of the bird giving in to Mary's protests. Mary's brother started teasing her all the time with comments like - "who has won the battle? Oh! you are losing ground against such a tiny bird? How can you accept defeat from such a tiny bird. The bird is so weak in comparison to you". As Mary's brother teased her with such comments, her anger increased.

Mary is teased

After a long time, one day, when Mary's brother came home, he found her in a very unusual, calm mood. He asked

The victorious bird - Gauri

her, "what has been the position of the fight to-day? It seems that, you have come to an understanding". To this Mary told her brother, "there is no question of an understanding, but, yes, the battle is over". Her brother replied "how has this situation come up?" There being no battle, he was not able to understand how the long drawn out battle could end. To this, Mary replied, "Oh come on, now I have been able to understand the value of effort and hard work. I used to get angry on the poor bird just for nothing. She has proved to be very brave. I have taken away my challenge to her as, I have realised that, those who work constantly and bravely can never be defeated". From that day, onwards, Mary allowed the bird to make its nest in her room. All the straws the bird dropped in the room would be lifted by Mary and thrown away. Mary named the bird Gauri, and let her develop her home in her room.

THERE IS NEVER DEFEAT FOR THE INDIVIDUALS WHO CONTINUE TO FOLLOW THEIR TARGETS

ANGER CAN KILL

Once upon a time, in the town of Varanasi, there was a pool. In that pool there lived two geese and one tortoise. These three were very good friends, and the tortoise among them was the one who talked too much.

Home of the three friends

Once it so happened that, there was no rain in Varanasi, and the pool in which the three friends lived, started getting dry. Then, the geese thought of moving to another pool which had enough water in it. One day, they went to the tortoise and told him of their plan to leave this home.

Let us change our home

When the tortoise heard the plan of the geese, he was upset, at, being left alone to pine in this dry pool. He asked the geese to take him too. The geese replied "how will we carry you?" He now suggested to them that, they should get a strong stick. This stick he would hold on to, and they would all fly off together to safety. The geese liked the plan but told the tortoise that he would have to keep quiet all the way, for, if he opened his mouth to talk, he would fall off the stick. This warning the geese had to give the tortoise because they knew that he talked too much. The plan was finalised, and the geese brought a big strong stick. The next day, they planned to leave. Soon the next morning came and the three friends were ready to take off to their new abode.

The tortoise held the stick from the middle and the geese caught it from two ends, and they all flew off as they had planned.

The three friends flying to safety

The fat tortoise was very heavy so, the geese could not fly too high. While they passed over a small township, some children who were playing on the roadside, saw the sight. The children shouted aloud, "Aha! what a lovely sight, but, surely the tortoise will fall as he is too fat". Another child said, "yes as soon as he falls, he will die, and then we will pick him up. He will be very good food".

When the tortoise heard all this being said about him,

The tortoise will soon fall

he felt very angry. In his anger, he opened his mouth to reply to them, and there, he really fell like a blob on the road and died at once. This happened because he got angry and wanted to reply back to the abusing children.

ALWAYS BE CALM AND QUIET.

NEVER BE GREEDY

Once upon a time there lived a dog. This dog used to stay in one street of the town, where someone or the other would give him some food. One day it so happened that, the dog could not get any food in his street. In search of food the dog went out of the street on to another street. Here he found a kind master who gave the hungry dog some bread and a bone of meat.

Having got enough food to eat, the dog ate the bread there only and, thought to himself that, the bone he would enjoy elsewhere. Thinking so, the dog moved away from that street, to look for a quieter place to enjoy the bone. As he was looking for a quiet place, he came across a stream.

Search ends

A stream ahead

While the dog was still standing near the stream, he saw his own shadow in the water of the stream. Thinking that there was another dog also with another bone. The dog thought why not snatch the other bone also and then eat them both at some quiet place.

Soon the temptation got over the dog's silence and he

Temptation ahead

The bone gets lost

barked on to the other dog-that was his own shadow in the water. Barking at the other dog he lost the bone in his mouth, which floated away in the flow of the water.

Besides losing his own bone, the dog could also not find the other dog in the water. In this way the greedy dog who wished to snatch another's bone lost his own also.

WE SHOULD NEVER BE GREEDY.

SHARING IS GOOD

Once upon a time there lived too goats in a village. These two goats were good friends. One day they both wanted to go to a garden to eat grass. Deciding to go to one garden, they both came out of the village.

On their way to the garden they had to cross a small river, by a very narrow bridge. Now they both started fighting, as to who would go first. One said that she would go first, while the other said that, she would go first. In this way they both continued fighting, standing near the bridge they had to cross.

Going out to eat-the two friends

Who should go first?

After a long time of fighting, they both decided that they would move together on that narrow bridge, neither was willing to be second.

They continued to move till they came to the centre of the bridge and, here they lost balance, and both of them fell in the river and lost their lives.

This is what happens when we do not have the sense to share. Just as the two goats fell in the river.

The goats off the bridge

Sharing a task to success

Another two goats came on the bridge. They also had to cross the bridge. Can you guess how these two goats crossed the bridge together and without fighting. You know what they did? One goat sat in the middle of the bridge, and, the other crossed over her back, and walked off. When one had passed so, the one who had sat, got up and also walked off. See how easy it was, when they knew how to share.

So, see how the second pair of goats crossed the same narrow bridge just because they were willing to share. The first pair of goats lost their lives just because they did not know how to share.

SHARING HELPS US TO ACHIEVE SUCCESSES.

THE PROUD PRINCESS

There was once, a very proud princess. The princess was very proud as, she was very beautiful.

The princess used to look at herself in the mirror all the time. She was very sure that no one or nothing could ever be more beautiful than her.

One day, as the princess was looking at the mirror as usual, she heard a voice saying aloud, "don't be proud of yourself and your beauty, as, there are many other things

The proud princess

in the world more beautiful than you are. Go to your garden pool and you will find out for yourself that you are not the most beautiful".

Hearing this, the proud princess was very angry and she at once got up, to go to the pool. She wanted to see who on earth could ever be more beautiful than her. When she went to the pool, she saw a beautiful pink lotus in full bloom in the centre of the lake. While she was still gazing at the flower, she heard the same voice again. This time the voice said, "this flower is more beautiful than you. This is because it gives joy to people and you give pleasure to none- you are too proud".

The beautiful lotus

Hearing this voice, the princess was very angry. She went home, and lay in bed sobbing. Soon night came and from the window peeped the beautiful full moon. She could also see the sparkling stars in the sky. While she was still admiring this beauty of the night sky, she again heard the same voice. The voice said to her, “the moon and the stars are more beautiful than you, they are not proud like you. They also give joy to people who look at them”. Hearing this the princess stopped sobbing, and sat in her bed thinking over it all.

Beauty of the night sky

The princess understanding the truth

After thinking for sometime the princess decided that now onwards, she would never be proud of herself, and she would try to give joy to others.

YOU ARE BEAUTIFUL ONLY IF YOU GIVE JOY TO OTHERS.

TO BE TOGETHER IS BEING STRONG

Once upon a time, there lived a woodcutter in a small village. The woodcutter had four sons, who all studied in the village school. All the four boys were good in their studies but, they were always fighting with each other. Whether they were at school, at home or on the road, they were always fighting with each other.

Seeing the boys fighting all the time was a cause of worry for the father, the woodcutter. He thought, "these sons of mine are always fighting with each other, how will they carry on my business together?" These thoughts often worried the woodcutter, and he often asked his friends to suggest ways and means by which he could make his sons realise that, they will never achieve anything if they continue fighting like this - among themselves. Many

Forever fighting

suggestions came from the friends of the woodcutter however, there was no real plan by which an end could be put to their fighting. This thought of a breaking home worried the woodcutter and he fell ill.

One day while he was lying and thinking of the same problem, an idea came to his mind. He called all the four sons. When they all came, he showed them a very huge bundle of wood. He asked each one of them to pick the bundle on his back. However the bundle was found to be very heavy by each one of them and none could lift it at all, not even an inch above the ground.

Test of strength

Seeing this, the woodcutter called all the four near him, and asked them to pick the bundle together. They all tried it together and lo! and behold! It was so very easily lifted. All the four sons were so surprised to see how easy the task was, when it was done by them all together.

Togetherness

Seeing this the children were very happy and now the woodcutter said to them, "see dears, each one of you tried to lift the bundle but, you could not. As soon as you all got together to do the task, it was so easily done. In the same way children, if you do any work together in unity, without fighting, you achieve your objective easily, just as you could lift the bundle of wood as soon as you did the task together". The boys understood the fact that, fighting helps no one, and that work done in togetherness is easily done.

From that day the four brothers left fighting with each other and became good friends, besides being brothers. They started sharing their happiness and troubles with each other. Now onwards they found it so easy to lift the burden of life together. They realised that happiness increases with togetherness, and troubles decrease with togetherness.

UNITY AND TOGETHERNESS BRINGS STRENGTH FOR ALL.

GOD CAN WORK WONDERS

Joseph was the favourite son of Jacob, who had many other sons also. Jacob used to shower favours on Joseph because he was his favourite son. This was not liked by the other sons of Jacob and, they felt very jealous of Joseph. Now can you tell why Joseph was the loved son of his father from among a number of sons. This is because, Joseph was a good child, an obedient son, and never did anything that was wrong. Besides, Joseph used to tell his father whatever wrong the other brothers also did. This is why Joseph was loved more than the other brothers.

Once, the ten brothers of Joseph went with their flocks of sheep about sixty miles away from their home. When they did not return as per their set plan, Jacob was worried, and he sent his son Joseph to see what had happened to his sons. After a long and tiring journey, at last, Joseph was able to meet his brothers.

Jacob's sons in the forest

When Joseph's brothers saw him coming towards them, they were very angry and felt jealous of him. Now a sense of hatred for Joseph kindled in their minds, and a wicked plan came to their minds. "We should kill him," they thought, and they all agreed to the proposal. One brother suggested, "let us not shed blood, we could throw him in a den or a hole and tell father that a wild beast attacked him". Still another brother suggested pointing to a pit or a well, "it would be better to put him there and let him starve". After a long debate on the issuc, all the brothers agreed to, throwing Joseph in a well. Soon enough they all attacked him, tied his hands and threw him in the well.

Joseph thrown in the well

Just as this drama was being enacted, there came a caravan of Indians who were going to Egypt to sell their spices. At once an idea occurred to one of the brothers that, they should sell Joseph to these merchants and thus get rid of him. This plan was discussed with the merchants, and they agreed to buy Joseph for 15 dollars. After the money was given to the brothers of Joseph, a rope was lowered down the well and Joseph was pulled out of the well. The merchants took hold of Joseph, tied him to the back of a camel and he moved away with the caravan.

Joseph sold

The wicked brothers had sold Joseph to serve as a slave to the Egyptians but, fate and God had something else in store for him.

When the brothers reached home they were asked by Jacob about the whereabouts of Joseph, and was sure that some wild beast had eaten his beloved son. The brothers of Joseph did not dare to tell the truth. Here, Jacob resigned to his fate of having lost his most loved son.

On the other hand, when Joseph reached Egypt, he was sold to a man, whose name was Potihar who was the captain of the guards in the service of the King of Egypt, and as such he was an important person in the country. It did not take long for Potihar to notice that, Joseph was his best and most trustworthy servant and soon, Joseph was put in charge of the entire household.

Here in the household, Potihar's wife played mischief with Joseph and, he was thrown in the prison. His good days were again lost however, good people do not really suffer. God helps them out of all the troubles they land in

Captain's instructions to Joseph

and HE has his own ways of doing so. At just this time there was a plot to poison the King of Egypt. This plot was suspected to have been made by the chief butler and chief baker. These two officers of the King's household were thus also put in prison, and Potihar asked Joseph to keep an eye on these new prisoners. Here in the prison, these two had dreams and the dreams were accurately interpreted by Joseph. After some time, when the King had two dreams, he also called for Joseph to interpret his dreams. The King's dreams were interpreted by Joseph like this. Joseph said that, in Egypt there would now be seven years of plenty, and then, seven years of famine. So Joseph suggested that, in the years of plenty, stocks of food could be hoarded for the days of famine. If this could be done, Joseph suggested that, the days of famine could be easily avoided. The King liked the plan and then appointed Joseph as the ruler of Egypt in order to plan out in the days of plenty how to avoid the days of famine.

God's reward for the good man Joseph

Thus the man Joseph who was thrown in a well to starve and die, became the King of Egypt. Such are the ways of God which we can not understand. God knows everything and plans everything. He always looks after his good children. The bad sons of Jacob were never heard of, while the good man Joseph was rewarded by the Almighty for his goodness. So children, goodness always gets its rewards. If man does not reward a good person there is God above to see what we do and reward us accordingly.

I HAVE TO BE GOOD, NO MATTER WHAT HAPPENS.

SHARING IS GREAT

Once upon a time, there was a man whose name was Gangudas. He lived in the town of Lahore and had a flourishing business. Life was very fine for Gangu, till one day, his business fell upon evil days, and his business suffered heavy losses. When Gangu was a rich merchant, he had a huge battalion of friends who stayed with him all the time and enjoyed his hospitality. However, when the same Gangu fell to bad luck, the same friends started laughing at him and scorning at him. Gangu tried very hard to come out of this fate but, when all was looking to be lost, he decided to meet a saint to solve his problem. He had heard that near his place there was a town by the name of Goindwal, and there in this town lived a saint Amar Das who would help people in distress. Gangu Das decided to meet this saint and seek for help.

One fine day, Gangu made his plan and set out to meet the saint at the town of Goindwal. On reaching Goindwal, Gangu was told that, he would be able to meet the Guru only if he took food at the Guru's langar, i.e. his free kitchen. He agreed to this condition and went to the kitchen.

However, when Gangu went to the kitchen, he saw that people of all castes and creeds were eating there. At first he was a bit reluctant but, he had to meet the Guru so, he decided that he will eat with the others. He said to himself, "I must give up my pride of caste, I must take food from this kitchen." Thinking of the necessity of eating, good sense prevailed and Gangu decided to eat with the others. After eating, Gangu was given the chance of meeting the Guru. Gangu fell at the feet of the Guru and told him his story of woe, and requested the Guru to help him. After hearing Gangu's story, the Guru told Gangu to go to Delhi where he could now start his new business.

Gangu at the kitchen

The Guru told Gangu that now, at Delhi his business would flourish and that he would become rich once again. With this blessing, the Guru warned Gangu that, he should not ever allow the success of his business enter his head.

The Guru said, “Gangu, always remember God, and always be ready to help the needy”.

He continued, “Gangu remember that it is God who gives us all success in all we do so never forget HIM, for, those who forget God become unhappy in the end”.

The blessings of the Guru

Gangu heard the advice of the Guru and agreed to live by it, and left the Guru's house very happily.

Now very soon Gangu left for Delhi, and there he started his new business. As the Guru had predicted, his business flourished, and Gangu became very wealthy once again. This wealth by and by turned the head of Gangu the merchant. One day a poor brahmin came to the home of Gangu with a letter from his Guru. The letter just read, "give this poor needy brahmin what he needs". Gangu asked the brahmin what is it that he needed. The brahmin told Gangu that, he was very poor and he had to marry his daughter. He said that he wanted some help from Gangu for the marriage of his daughter. The Guru had sent him to Gangu for financial help.

The Guru's letter

Gangu did not really like this act of his Guru and thought to himself, "I have earned my wealth with my hard work. If I give money to this man, the Guru will send more and more men for such help. I should not entertain such a request". Thinking so to himself, Gangu refused to help the brahmin. The brahmin felt very unhappy about this treatment, and returned disappointed to the Guru. The Guru gave the brahmin the money he needed and was surprised to hear about the behaviour of Gangu.

After some days, Gangu's luck once again turned against him, and he began to suffer losses in his business. This took no time to make Gangu poor all over again. Very soon, Gangu realised that, "most certainly, bad luck has come back to me because of my bad behaviour with the old brahmin". He thought that he must go to the brahmin and ask him for his forgiveness.

IT IS GOOD TO SHARE BECAUSE IT MAKES MORE PEOPLE HAPPY.

TO LOVE IS DIVINE

In a jungle there was a grove of bunyan trees. In the midst of this grove there was one big, yes, the biggest of all the bunyan trees. On the top of this tree lived a pair of crows, and, at the bottom of this same tree lived a poisonous snake who was also very huge in size.

This serpent lived here on this tree, and lo! and behold! he thrived on the eggs and babies of the crow couple. As time passed, the raids of the serpent became more frequent, and not even one baby crow would now escape his eyes.

This situation made the crow couple very unhappy, and, having lost a number of babies, one day, the mother crow fell at the feet of the father crow and said, "My dear, in this way, we will always continue to lose our offspring.

The unhappy neighbours

Let us shift from here and make a home for ourselves in some other tree, in another grove". The love of her lost children made her cry aloud and she said, "if this continues, all our children will also be destroyed in the future by this evil serpent. How can we ever be happy on this tree, when we continue to live in the fear of the serpent". The mother crow continued to cry and pleaded to the father crow to move from this tree because, here, she felt all that she loved was in danger, her children, her husband and her home. She felt that, all this would be destroyed in times to come and continued to weep aloud. However, even after continued pleading the father crow could not be convinced he said, "Oh, my beloved, what do you ask me to do? To move from this tree where we have lived for so long? It is here we were both born, it is here that we grew into adults, it is in the midst of these growths we got married. How can we forget those beautiful moments of our lives and leave this tree, just for the sake of this serpent? How can we leave our birthplace, how can we leave our motherland, and go to take abode elsewhere? Oh! no, I cannot think of doing such a thing just because of a little danger. How can we leave our country and our countrymen?" Hearing this, mother crow started crying once again still louder than before and saying "yes your countrymen, your country-love for all but what about my love for my husband and my children who are always in danger?" Now, the father crow heard this appeal and tried to console the mother crow, "do not worry, I shall think of ways and means of solving the problem of the serpent. I shall see what I can do to save ourselves from the danger of this neighbour of ours. Wise men say that, there is no evil in destroying an evil. I have some learned friends who are well versed in law and politics. I will go to them, consult them, and see how fast we can destroy this serpent".

Saying this to his wife, the father crow went to meet and seek the advice of his friend, the Jackal, who is known for his cunning.

The friends meet

After hearing the story of the father crow, the Jackal told him, “friend do not worry, I shall surely think of a solution for your problem. You must stop fretting and let me think for a while”.

Saying this, the jackal sat in a quiet and thoughtful mood. After some moments of thinking, the jackal said, “Ha! Ha! I have got a solution. You will soon be able to destroy the serpent for the sake of your love. Now listen to what I have to say”. He continued,“do you see the tank there? To this tank, the rich merchant’s wife comes to bathe every day, as, this is the merchant’s private tank. Here, before starting her bath, she removes her heavy diamond jewellery, and puts it all near the tank. You just see when she comes and, as soon as she has removed the necklace, and placed it near the tank, you just remove the necklace and fly with it and throw it into the snake’s hole. However friend, be careful that, the maids of the merchant’s wife see where you go. Then they will follow you, and, to take the necklace from the hole will have to kill the serpent”.

The crow liked the plan, and flew off, to execute it as

Scene set for the Crow's action

soon was possible. The crow now came to the tank and sat on a high branch of the tree, waiting to see the merchant's wife coming there. Soon enough, the merchant's wife came followed by some maids. She was loaded with jewels. The merchant's wife came close to the tank, and in making herself ready for the bath, she removed her big diamond necklace and put it near the tank, and then slipped in for a bath. As soon as the merchant's wife went into the tank for the bath, the crow gave a quick dive, picked the necklace and flew away with it, with all the maids just watching helplessly. Few people even followed the flight of the crow and noticed where exactly he had dropped the necklace. They saw that the necklace was dropped into the hole of the trunk of a bunyan tree, and that was the exact place where the serpent lived. These people went back and brought men and appliances to dig the necklace from the hole in which it had been dropped.

Merchant's men in action

These people finally dug the hole deep and also did succeed in killing the serpent. After this, the crows were left in peace to live in their beloved motherland, the bunyan tree, comfortably and secure for ever after.

Love is a great treasure that we should all cherish, and serve as much as we can. The crow did not leave the bunyan tree that had been his birthplace, and the forest that was his country, just because of some problem in there. He tried to solve his problem and make himself safe and comfortable in his own land and home.

WE MUST LOVE ALL THAT IS OURS.

HONESTY IS THE BEST POLICY

Once upon a time there was a woodcutter who used to earn a living by cutting wood from the forest and selling it in the town. In this way, he used to earn just enough with which he could feed his family and himself.

One day the woodcutter met a friend who told him that, he could get some fine wood near a stream nearby. His friend told him, "this wood near the stream is of better quality, and would thus sell for more money". Hearing this, the woodcutter decided to go to this new woodland, near the stream shown to him by his friend. When he reached the new forest, oh! what a delight he felt, "this wood is really of a very fine quality, the sahibs in town will buy it for their furniture". Thinking so to himself, the woodcutter sat on top of a tree and started chopping off branches and

The woodcutter at his job

I have lost my axe even

twigs before, he could come to hit the thicker trunk itself.

He had hardly started his work that, the axe fell into the stream and, oh! what misery surrounded the poor woodcutter. He lamented, “I had come here with the hope of earning more but alas! I have lost my only axe”. Saying this to himself, he came down from the tree and sat on the ground thinking of what he could do now.

While he was still thinking of his bad luck, he saw a miracle of God. In the middle of the stream he saw a figure as if of God.

The figure called out to him and said, “why do you worry friend, I have brought your axe from the stream”. On hearing this voice, the woodcutter was very happy and ran

The miracle of God

to the stream to take his axe.

As he reached close to the stream, the figure there showed to him an axe of gold, and said, “come and take your axe. Take it and continue your work”. Seeing the axe from close, the woodcutter was very disappointed and said, “oh no Sir, this axe is not mine, this axe is made of gold”. Hearing this, the figure in the stream disappeared in the stream. The woodcutter had hardly turned his back to the stream utterly disheartened that, the movement in the water of the stream could be heard once again.

At once the woodcutter turned to the stream but, once again there was disappointment for him. This time the same figure appeared once again, this time showing the woodcutter a silver axe in his hand. The man in the stream said, “friend I went back into the stream and I have found another axe from there, this silver axe this time. I am sure this must be yours”. “Oh no Sir”, the woodcutter said again “please take this away and try to look for my axe if you can”. Hearing this, the man in the stream

The brooding woodcutter

disappeared once again, and the woodcutter being extremely unhappy returned to the tree. Here he started fretting and saying to himself in utter distress, " I will never again get back my axe and I have no money to buy another. I do wonder how I will earn my livelihood now".

While the woodcutter was still depressed and unhappy, to his great surprise, he saw the man of the stream come and stand in front of him. This mystery man held an ordinary axe in his hand, and he gave it to the woodcutter and said, "Now, is this your axe? This is the last one I could find in the depths of the stream".

Seeing the axe, the woodcutter was very excited and said, "Aha! yes Sir, this is my axe. Thank you so much my lord, I thank you very much". Saying this, the woodcutter took the axe from the figure and was very happy.

The happy woodcutter

Giving the axe to the woodcutter the figure said, "you have shown honesty and, inspite of being so very poor, you did not get tempted by gold and silver, so, God who sees everything, has rewarded your honesty. Go home, and from to day, you will have a beautiful palace to live in, and the life of a king is yours now. Throw the axe for ever now. Now you are a prince to live in a palace for all time. Your honesty has been seen by God and HE has rewarded you for it".

LEARN TO BE HAPPY WITH WHAT YOU HAVE.

THE FOUR FRIENDS

Once upon a time, by a lake, in a forest, there lived four friends. They were, a small brown mouse, who had big black eyes and a long tail. He lived in a hole on the bank of the lake. The second friend was a jet black crow who lived on the Jamun tree close by. The third friend was a tortoise who lived in the lake and was very happy there. The fourth friend was a beautiful deer with large eyes and a golden coat with white spots. These four friends were very happy living together, as they lived peacefully and no one ever troubled them.

The four friends

Once it so happened that the Mouse, the Crow, and the Tortoise met beside the lake, waiting for their friend the deer. When, even after a long wait, the deer did not come home they were all worried and the Mouse said, “there must be something wrong with our friend the deer, he must be in some trouble, or a hunter must have trapped him”. To this suggestion all the three friends agreed and the crow flew off to the forest to look for the deer. The crow flew here and there through the length and breadth of the forest, looking for his friend the deer. He flew on and on, crying aloud, "deer, deer my friend where are you?" After having spent some time in the forest at last the crow could hear at one spot, a faint voice calling, "Help, I am here, Oh! help me". The crow could spot the place from where the voice was coming and he came down to where the deer was, saying, "Oh! there you are my dear friend I have been looking for you everywhere. Oh! so you have been trapped in the hunter's net?"

Amazed at the situation in which the deer was, the crow asked the deer, "friend, shall I fly back to our friends and see what all of us can do to free you from here". "Oh! please do dear friend, please do something and very quickly". The crow thus flew to where his friends were.

Now the crow flew back to the lake and told the other three friends about all that had transpired between him and the deer. He told the others, "I have found our friend but, he is in great danger. He is trapped in a hunter's net". They had hardly heard the news that, the tortoise said "the mouse can cut the net and free our friend". The mouse replied "yes I can, but, how to reach there?" Now

At last I have found you

In service of a friend

the crow come to their help, and suggested, “I can carry you on my back”. The idea was very good and, at once the mouse jumped on the back of the crow and they flew off.

Very soon they both reached the place where the deer was lying tied up in the hunter’s nest. At once, the mouse jumped from the back of the crow and started his work of cutting the net. Soon in a few moments, the deer was free. Just then, the tortoise also joined them, and they were very happy to be together once again. Just as they were enjoying their togetherness, they heard a distant sound of someone coming through the forest. They were sure it was the hunter. At once the crow flew away, the mouse got into a hole, and the deer ran away very fast and was soon out of sight. However, the slow tortoise was left to move slowly towards a bush where he would hide. In the meantime, the hunter was there, and was shocked to see that, his net was empty, and the deer had escaped. However, while he was looking around for the deer, the hunter saw the tortoise who, being very slow had not been able to hide in the bushes. As the slow tortoise was crawling to the bush, the hunter caught him and was happy that, at least he had got a tortoise for a meal. He quickly grabbed the tortoise put him in a bag and went off. The crow, who was still sitting at the top of the tree had seen all this occur, and, he called the other friends shouting this "Oh! Mouse, Oh! Deer, come quickly, now our friend the tortoise is in danger". As soon as they both came out of their hideouts, the crow told them that, the hunter had taken the tortoise in his bag. Now friends, he asked "what can we do to set our friend the tortoise free from the danger he is in?" The deer said "I know what to do. I shall go and stand in the path of the hunter, pretending to be eating grass. As soon as he sees me, he will surely drop the bag, and run after me. Then the mouse can cut open the bag and the tortoise will be free. "But suppose the hunter catches you", the crow said. The deer replied "Oh! do not worry about that, I can run very fast". This plan was approved by the three friends. Now, the deer calmly stood in the path of the hunter

Hunter trying for a better dinner

pretending to be eating grass. The hunter saw the deer. He at once dropped the bag and ran after the deer. Now, the mouse quickly cut open the bag, and set free the tortoise. On the other hand the deer ran so fast that, the hunter could not catch it, and soon he stopped running after it.

The unlucky hunter with empty bag

Thinking it to be hopeless, the hunter decided that he should be happy with the little tortoise for to-day. Thinking so, he returned to where he had left the bag with the tortoise in it. As soon as he reached there, he found the bag empty, and could not believe his eyes. "What, no tortoise? How did it escape? How unlucky I am. First the deer escaped and now the tortoise. Even this slow creature has been able to escape. Now there will be no dinner for me tonight". The tortoise, the deer the mouse and the crow quietly watched the hunter as he went away with his empty bag in his hand.

THE GREEDY LOSE MORE AND GAIN LESS.

LEARN TO FORGIVE

Once upon a time there were two very good and dear friends - their names were Dharam and Papi. They both lived in a village near the town of Vaishali. Dharam, as the name shows, was a very good and innocent young man, while Papi was too smart and somewhat vicious of nature. They were both farmers in the village. One year, it so happened that, there was very little rain in the area and they both found it very difficult to earn enough for a living.

One day, Papi thought of a plan and came to Dharam, and asked him, "dear friend do you earn enough to maintain your family?"

To this question, Dharam replied, "no friend not at all. We are finding it very difficult to get even two meals a day. Can you suggest any way by which we can earn more?" To this Papi replied, "yes, I have a plan. This is a small village and here, we cannot expect to earn more. I suggest that we

Plans of Vaishali

go to the nearby town Vaishali. I hear that, in big towns there is a lot to do. Let us go to Vaishali and look for some work". To this suggestion, Dharam gave his approval.

After a few days the two men, Dharam, and Papi, good friends, decided to leave for Vaishali.

With high hopes of a good livelihood, the two friends went to Vaishali. On reaching the town, they both started looking for jobs, and, as luck favoured them, they both got good jobs. They both started working on their new jobs and they were happy and comfortable.

However, after a few days only, the loving Dharam remembered his family, and wanted to return to his home in the village. One day, he told his friend Papi, "come on friend, now we have both earned quite a lot of money, let us return home and live with our families". To this, Papi agreed. Soon after, they both left Vaishali for their village.

While they were on their way home, a wicked idea came to the mind of Papi. He told Dharam that, it was not

Dharam and Papi returning home

safe to carry so much wealth with them. Robbers and dacoits may take away all that they had earned. The idea was very reasonable, and so, Dharam agreed to the suggestion. Dharam said, "Yes friend what you say is correct, but, what should we do?"

Papi thought for a while and then said, "Aha! friend, I have got an idea, let us dig a hole, deep enough to put in it our bags of wealth. We will carry home a little, and, whenever we need more, we can come and take it out of this hole. No one knows about it except you and me".

Digging their wealth

The innocent Dharam liked the idea, and both of them got busy digging a deep hole, at the root of a tree. When the hole was deep enough, they both put their bags in it and covered the hole and went off.

After a few days, they reached their homes in the village. Their families were very happy to receive them. Now that, they had earned enough, life became comfortable for their families and they were all happy. While life was smiling at them, one day, a wicked idea came to the mind of Papi. He thought of going to the tree, and taking out both the bags dug in, and thus cheat his friend. The next day, Papi went out to the forest. When he reached the tree, he started digging and, lo! and behold! he was ever so happy when he saw the two bags full of coins in front of him, one belonging to him, and the other Dharam's. While he just bent to pick the bags, he heard some noise, so, he picked just one bag, and quickly closed the hole again. At once he planned that, to take away the other bag, he would again come the next night. Thinking so, he moved homewards.

However, bad thoughts and bad actions never succeed. While Papi was on his way, a gang of robbers attacked him, and robbed him of his bag of riches. They also beat him severely, and left him wounded. Next day when Papi had not returned home, his family worried. When Dharam came to know, he set out to look for him.

Dharam comes to meet Papi

Dharam thought to himself, “may be Papi wanted some money”, so he went to see him in the jungle. Dharam went towards the jungle to look for his dear friend Papi. He had gone for just a few miles that, he saw Papi lying wounded on the jungle road. As soon as Papi saw Dharam come to his rescue, he burst into tears and told him, that, he had come with an idea of stealing both the bags of money. On the way he was caught by thieves and left there wounded. Papi also told Dharam that, the thieves had taken away the bag he was carrying, and left him there on the jungle road badly wounded. On hearing Papi’s story, Dharam forgave Papi for his evil thoughts and intentions. He, as a good friend of Papi, also promised to share his wealth with Papi. In this way, after having lovingly consoled his wicked friend, he took him safely to his home.

The result of Papi’s greed for both the bags of riches ended in Papi having lost his one bag also. However, he was very lucky that he had a good and loving friend like Dharam. We should never be greedy as, there is no end to greed. Greed always ends up in losses. I must always forgive a friend, even if he does something against me.

A GOOD FRIEND SHOULD ALWAYS FORGIVE HIS FRIEND.

ALWAYS KEEP GOOD COMPANY

Once upon a time there was a small boy, whose name was Karan. Karan was a very good boy, and was very happy at school. His teachers also liked him a lot as, he was good in studies, and was also a very quiet and obedient child. Life was going on very well for this child, who was very happy and liked by all.

One day, while Karan was playing, he met another boy, whose name was Vikrant. In a short time, Karan and Vikrant became good friends. Little knowing that Vikrant was a naughty boy, Karan's friendship with him became deep, and the two started playing together, and, Karan soon also started learning all the bad habits of Vikrant.

The lovable child Karan

The new friends

As time went on, the two boys became very close to each other, and, the good boy Karan started giving less attendance at his school, and getting more and more involved with playing and learning bad habits of his friend Vikrant. His schedule was that, at school time Karan would come out of home, and join Vikrant somewhere on some road, and play with him for the whole day, and at school time would return home. In this way, weeks passed by till at last, one of Karan's teachers brought this to the notice of the Principal. The Principal sent the teacher to Karan's house to make the relevant enquiries about the situation. The teacher came to Karan's house to ask his mother why Karan was not attending school. Karan's mother was shocked to hear that, Karan had not attended school for the last one month, though he was going to school every day. After making some enquiries, Karan's mother came to know that her son had got into bad company. She thought of a plan to teach Karan a lesson.

In the evening when Karan came home, his mother asked him to bring one kilogram of apples from the market. The apples were brought and kept in a tray. In the middle of these apples, she kept one rotten apple, and

The bad company

then asked Karan to keep the tray away. In the morning when fruits were to be served at the breakfast table, Karan's mother asked him to bring the tray of the apples. Lo! and Behold! what did they see? They noticed that, the apples close to the rotten apple had also got spoiled - so one rotten apple had spoiled four other good apples, as, they had been too close to the rotten apples. Now the mother showed Karan how, a single rotten apple can destroy other good apples that remain close to the bad ones. In this way, she told Karan that, he should not keep bad company as, bad company can destroy the best of us.

This is why it is said by elders that, you should always keep good company. Bad company spoils a person and it becomes difficult to become good once again.

BAD COMPANY SPOILS A PERSON.

THE DUTIFUL DONKEY

Once upon a time there was washerman whose name was Kalpa. Like all other washermen, Kalpa also had a donkey to carry the loads of clothes. Kalpa also had a dog to look after the safety of these clothes of the customers, and of course Kalpa's house.

Life was being very kind to Kalpa and it was very comfortable for all the three of Kalpa's family, Kalpa, his donkey and the dog. They were all busy and happy in their daily routines and worked very sincerely and regularly. Just at this time, Lady Luck decided otherwise.

Kalpa's friends

One night when the washerman was asleep after the day's work, and the donkey and the dog were sitting out of the house, a band of robbers came to rob the washerman's house and even kill him. The robbers were standing in front of Kalpa's house, and planning their strategy of the attack. The donkey saw them standing and talking, so he suspected foul play. At once he became alert, and told the dog, "friend these men are robbers and it seems as if they

Why should I bark?

are going to attack our master. Friend, our master's life and property are in danger. I suggest that, you bark loudly so that these robbers run away, and our master also gets alerted". To this suggestion, the dog turned a deaf ear. Seeing this, the donkey repeated the request to the dog by saying, "friend, why are you so quiet, why don't you bark and wake the master? If you bark, the master will be alerted, and the robbers will also run away...." When the donkey had said these words several times, the dog got enraged and said, "Oh what do I care, let the master be robbed. Lately, I have stopped being dutiful because, I am not getting any return for it. He has reduced my food, so, as he is not giving me enough return, I will also not do my duty for him. I do not care what these robbers do to my master and his property. I am not going to bark, no matter what you tell me and how much you tell me".

So saying, the dog just turned his back to the robbers and slept as if he was most unconcerned. The donkey, on the other hand, feeling duty-bound, once again tried to convince the dog of his duty and said, "Oh, what a servant you are and what a friend of the master, even when your master is in danger, you are not doing your duty, just because you say that, there is no reward" - what a villain you are. Saying this to the dog the donkey thought to himself "what should I do to help the master, these robbers are all ready for the attack on my master. Alright if this dog refuses to alert the master, I shall try to do so". Thinking so, the donkey started braying aloud, hoping that this would awaken the master. It happened just as it was expected, and, as soon as the donkey started braying, the robbers ran away, but, the noise also woke the master. Kalpa came out to see what the matter was, and seeing that, there was no obvious cause for the donkey to bray, he gave a thrashing to the dutiful donkey, for disturbing Kalpa's sleep.

Seeing this, the dog was very happy, and said to the donkey, "see dear friend donkey, this is the fate of the dutiful, in the hands of their masters. You were telling me to do my duty - Ha! Ha!

The return for doing duty

The donkey did cry in pain and was very hurt also yet, he thought that, he had done the right thing. He was pained but, he had been right in doing his duty - and also saved his master, is that not enough? The dog scorned the donkey and they both slept.

The robbers having been frightened that night, decided to once again try robbing the washerman, the next night. So, the next night, the same gang of robbers came again to Kalpa's house, at the dead of night. This night again, the donkey and the dog heard them discussing the strategy of attack. On the other hand, the donkey was wondering how he would warn the master now. While the robbers and the donkey were both busy planning their plans of action, there came to be heard the whistles of the police. The police was in search of this gang of robbers, and so they surrounded them and caught them.

Hearing noises near his house, Kalpa woke up and came out of his house to see what it was all about. Seeing the police and a few others there, Kalpa asked them what the matter was. Kalpa said to them, "why are you making

Robbers are caught

so much noise near my house?" To this a police constable replied, "Sir, we have been in search of these robbers in the city. To-night they had come to rob you and kill you also. Last night also they had come here with this plan of breaking into your house and killing you but, they were frightened by the braying of your donkey, and so we missed them last night. Tonight we have succeeded in catching them while they were just planning the attack on you and your house".

At once Kalpa realised that, last night this must have been the cause of the donkey's bray and "Oh, I gave him such a beating for the very good work he did". The washerman realised that, he had been unkind to the donkey and at once felt bad, and went to pat him on his back. From the next day, the donkey got his reward, as, he was given less work and more food. On the other hand, the dog who had not done his duty, and only complained about getting no return, got still less food, and was kept chained all the time.

WE SHOULD DO OUR DUTY BECAUSE IT IS OUR DUTY AND NOT BECAUSE WE MUST GET A RETURN.